NORTH-WEST RAILS IN COLOUR

by

PAUL SHANNON

Published by Platform 5 Publishing Ltd., Lydgate House, Lydgate Lane, Sheffield S10 5FH, England.

Printed in England by Finchmark Ltd., Unit 1, Ashton Road, Bredbury, Stockport, SK6 2QN.

ISBN 1 872524 35 4

INTRODUCTION

The last twenty years have arguably seen greater changes in the railway environment than any comparable period since the railways' birth. The slimmed-down system which emerged from the Beeching era still displayed many traditional features – such as station goods yards, semaphore signalling and loose-coupled freight trains – which only succumbed to modernisation in the seventies and eighties. This book aims to present a cross-section of railway views from North West England recorded on film during that period, with the emphasis on the last five years. I have not attempted to cover every class of locomotive, nor every section of the network; areas which see a wide variety of traffic or which abound in scenery – or both, such as the Cumbrian stretch of the West Coast main line – will merit more extensive coverage than those areas with less photographic potential.

Today's passenger railway in the North West has two focuses. For InterCity, the focus is undoubtedly the West Coast main line, which still carries a significant volume of Anglo–Scottish traffic as well as heavy loadings between the North West and points further south. For Regional Railways, the urban centres of Manchester and Merseyside provide an obvious focus, though the same organisation is of course responsible for providing cross-country and rural services through the North West. Almost all InterCity trains are electrically hauled for at least part of their journey, with diesel haulage limited to peripheral routes such as Preston–Blackpool and a handful of InterCity 125-operated services to Scotland. It is perhaps difficult to muster much enthusiasm for the various breeds of diesel and electric multiple-units operated by Regional Railways, but quite apart from their cost-effectiveness and therefore their ability to keep marginal services going, many of them have visual attractiveness by virtue of their livery – almost everything from standard blue and grey to Cornish chocolate and cream! Locomotive haulage returned to some longer-distance routes such as Manchester–Cardiff in the 1980s, but these in turn were ousted by Sprinters as soon as enough serviceable units became available. In Manchester recurring shortages of Pacers and Sprinters led to frequent loco-hauled substitution – sometimes rostered, sometimes not! – and at the time of writing rakes of smartly repainted hauled stock hauled by Class 37/4s are providing welcome relief from overcrowded units on peak-hour trains to Southport and Blackpool.

Freight workings in the North West have undergone radical change during the last twenty years. The once ubiquitous Class 25s and 40s are now just memories, and relentless rationalisation has brought about the closure of many yards, terminals and sidings. Nevertheless large quantities of freight are still carried, especially on the West Coast main line and around Manchester, Liverpool and the Peak District. All the divisions of Trainload Freight are represented in the North West, with regular flows including coal to Fiddlers Ferry, steel from Scotland to Wales, roadstone from Peak Forest and oil from Stanlow. Class 60s were beginning to make regular appearances on coal and roadstone workings in 1991, and the coming months will doubtless see further 'cascading' of older types as the 60s take hold of the most lucrative traffic flows. Pairs of Class 20s were still working from such places as Bickershaw and Parkside in late 1991, but surely not for much longer. Railfreight Distribution, too, is well represented in the North West, with container traffic to and from Trafford Park, Garston and Seaforth as well as several services passing through on their way to or from Scotland. A number of chemical flows operate to and from industrial plants in Cheshire, and most low-volume traffic formerly carried by Speedlink has been successfully accommodated on new company trains. Trip workings were not abolished entirely when Speedlink closed down, and there are still some delights for the patient enthusiast, such as wagonloads of starch from the Trafford Park industrial estate in Manchester.

I am grateful to all the photographers who contributed to this volume, especially those who kindly supplied the older material which gives some fascinating glimpses in the early days of 'modern' traction. I hope that the reader enjoys the pictorial tour of the North West.

Paul Shannon, Bolton November 1991

Front cover: Class 37/4 No. 37416 passes Kearsley with the 17.14 Manchester Victoria–Blackpool North commuter service on 8th August 1991, displaying the freshly repainted Mk 2A/B coaches which were regarded by some observers as a revival of the Lancashire & Yorkshire Railway 'club train' tradition. *Paul Shannon*

Rear cover: Class 24 No. 24133 passes Daresbury with 8F31, the 16.12 Croes Newydd–Warrington mixed goods train on 23rd June 1975. Most of the Class 24 fleet was withdrawn between August 1975 and December 1976, but No. 24133 survived in capital stock until March 1978. *Brian Roberts*

Right: Household coal traffic declined sharply in the 1980s, and by the end of the decade only four depots in North West England were still receiving deliveries by rail – at Birkenhead, Preston Deepdale, Blackburn and Carlisle. By mid 1991 only Birkenhead and Blackburn had timetabled services, with the other two depots being served by block trains as re- quired. A special 16.50 Washwood Heath–Preston Deepdale coal train is pictured arriving at Walton Old Junction, Warrington, on 27th June 1991, headed by Railfreight Distribution Class 47 No. 47214. The coal in this case had come from Gwaun-cae-Gurwen, Markham Main, Calver- ton and Gedling.

Paul Shannon

Left: After the mass transfer of Class 50s to the Western Region in May 1974, fifteen examples were retained in the North West for a further two years, hauling passenger and freight trains on the non-electrified routes from Preston and often appearing on the Settle to Carlisle line. No. 50031 is pictured at Dent Head with 7A09, the 09.32 Carlisle–Willesden wagonload service, on 7th May 1975. Its transfer to the Western Region came almost exactly a year later, and withdrawal took place on 21st July 1991, though with hopes held out for preservation.

Brian Roberts

Right: Whilst the Class 50s have spent most of their working lives on the Western and Southern regions, their earliest duties were concentrated on the northern half of the West Coast main line, where they provided interim traction on Anglo-Scottish expresses prior to the completion of electrification. From May 1970 the principal daytime trains were booked for double-heading in order to ensure smooth passage over Shap and Beattock summits, or – as in this illustration – over the notorious Long Drag. Nos. 50044 and 50009 pass Ais Gill with the diverted 14.00 Glasgow Central–London Euston on 14th April 1974. These locomotives were later named 'Exeter' and 'Conqueror' respectively, and coincidentally they were withdrawn from service on the same day, 11th January 1991. *John Cooper-Smith*

English Electric Type 4 locomotives, or Class 40s as they later became, quarter of a century. When new they were a common sight on express passenger services on the West Coast main line, and a batch of them even received names of Atlantic liners in recognition of the fact that they worked boat trains to Liverpool. Type 4 No. D 381, later to become Class 40 No 40181, heads south from Wigan with the daily express from Glasgow and Edinburgh to Birmingham New Street on Sunday 13th June 1965.

Michael Mensing

The BRCW Calder Valley units, later designated Class 110, were among the more distinctive first-generation DMU designs. As well as operating between Manchester and Bradford via the Calder Valley, they had regular duties on secondary routes on both sides of the Pennines, and after closure of the Woodhead route to passenger traffic, Calder Valley units were chosen for the replacement Manchester–Sheffield express service via the Hope Valley, where they were regarded as a poor substitute for the electric-hauled trains which they replaced. A three-car unit is pictured just east of Pemberton on 13th June 1965, forming the 6.5 p.m. departure from Liverpool Exchange to Bradford Exchange   *Michael Mensing*

Above: The entire Class 76 (formerly Class EM1) fleet was maintained at Reddish, along with the eight Class 506 EMUs formerly used on Manchester–Glossop–Hadfield local services. A visit to Reddish depot on 16th May 1976 finds Nos. 76031, 76010 and 76012 stabled there for the weekend. The jumper cables on No. 76031 show that it was one of the batch of Class 76s capable of working in multiple (and also fitted with train air brakes) for hauling trans-Pennine merry-go-round coal trains.

Right: A quartet of Class 40s, Nos. 40107, 40136, 40171 and 40135, is stabled at Edge Hill servicing depot on Sunday 21st September 1975. The gathering includes three out of the four green-liveried Class 40s in service at that time – and the fourth one was No. 40106, numerically not far from blue-liveried No. 40107!

Brian Roberts (2)

Above: Class 25 No. 25043 has just passed the site of Appleton station on the now-closed Widnes–St Helens line with 4F27, the 18.45 Wavertree–Wigan North Western parcels working on 6th May 1975. This train took a curious route via Ditton Junction, Widnes West Deviation Junction and Ravenhead Junction, regaining the direct Liverpool–Wigan line at St Helens Shaw Street. Behind the locomotive is one of the huge fleet of Southern Railway design parcels vans which operated throughout the BR system in the 1970s. *Brian Roberts*

Right: A mixed rake of BG and GUV parcels vans passes Brindle Heath sidings on its way to Red Bank carriage sidings on the afternoon of 12th September 1981, hauled by Class 40 No. 40092. The Brindle Heath area boasted a fine array of semaphores in 1981, controlling access to sidings on both sides of the line and also protecting the junction at Agecroft. Today Agecroft is no longer a junction, and the Tarmac stone terminal at Brindle Heath (visible to the right of the locomotive) has been mothballed, but the siding in the foreground still sees regular use at the time of writing for refuse trains to Appley Bridge. *Paul Shannon*

Left: The Metrovick Co–Bos began their careers on a variety of main-line and suburban duties including London St. Pancras–Manchester expresses, the Condor overnight fast freight service and commuter trains to and from Moorgate in the city of London. After a few years, however, they were relegated to secondary duties in North West England, centred on Barrow-in-Furness. All twenty Co–Bos were withdrawn from service between December 1967 and September 1968, only just outliving some of the steam traction which they had come to replace. The only Co–Bo to receive blue livery, No. D 5701, is seen near Grange-over-Sands with an up oil train on 21st June 1968.

Michael Mensing

Right: The unique centre-cab Clayton Type 1s are usually associated with Scotland, but the class had regular workings in Northern England on both sides of the Pennines. No. D 8515 makes its way towards Parton on the freight-only branch from Lowca on 20th June 1968, having taken a rake of wagons up the branch for loading. This stretch of line, which formed part of a through route from Parton to Distington and Ullock Junction, was closed in 1973. No D 8515 was consigned to the scrapheap in September 1971.

Michael Mensing

Typical of the wagonload freight services that used the Settle and Carlisle line in the 1970s and early 1980s is the lengthy Carlisle-bound train, pictured passing Dent station on the evening of 5th August 1981. The motive power is Class 40 No. 40184, which was latterly based at Longsight until its withdrawal in December 1982. Dent station was officially reopened to passenger traffic in July 1986, after a spell of seasonal use by privately sponsored excursion trains.   *Paul Shannon*

Class 40 No. 40038 leaves the Padiham branch at Rose Grove West Junction with a rake of empty 16-ton mineral wagons on 7th November 1975. The train is 8E49, the 14.55 Padiham–Healey Mills empties. Coal traffic to Padiham had gone over to road haulage by the early 1980s but made an unexpected return to the rail mode in November 1991 when Trainload Coal ran an experimental service from Maryport.

Brian Roberts

Left: In their twilight years the 'Deltics' made a few forays across the Pennines on cross-country services to and from Liverpool. Class 55 No. 55022 'ROYAL SCOTS GREY' restarts after a signal check near Broad Green with the 08.50 York–Liverpool service on 17th December 1981. No. 55022 was withdrawn from Eastern Region operating stock just after two weeks after the date of this photograph. *Brian Roberts*

Right: Class 37 No. 37067 rounds the curve at Buxworth with empty PCV cement tanks for Earles Sidings on 25th January 1984. Wagons of this type remained in use until the late 1980s on services from Earles Sidings to Widnes and Dewsbury, as well as on Scottish flows from Oxwellmains. No. 37067 was refurbished and ballasted in 1987 to become Class 37/7 No. 37703, and it has worked since then from Cardiff Canton depot as a member of the Trainload Coal fleet. *Brian Roberts*

Class 25 No. 25106 arrives at Great Rocks Junction with 6H42, the 08.21 Oakleigh–Tunstead limestone empties on 4th July 1983. The flow of industrial limestone from Tunstead quarry to Lostock and Oakleigh chemical plants near Northwich is one of the best known and longest established freight flows in the Buxton area, and the fact that some of the wagons still used today were originally built in the 1930s is a testimony to their good design and to ICI's careful maintenance of them over the years. The use of single Class 25 locomotives on Tunstead–Oakleigh serices lasted until 1984, after which there were spells of haulage by pairs of Class 20s, pairs of Class 37s and single Class 47s.   *Paul Shannon*

Class 76 No. 76021 heads an eastbound trainload of HTV hopper wagons past Torside on the now closed and lifted Woodhead route, on 1st June 1978. The Woodhead route benefited from gentler gradients than other trans-Pennine lines and boasted Great Britain's newest main-line tunnel, opened in 1954, but its non-standard electrification and life-expired high-voltage feeder cabling were factors which contributed to its untimely closure in July 1981. Most of the traffic which once used the Woodhead route was diverted via Diggle, but much of it disappeared because of changing circumstances.

Hugh Ballantyne

Right: In the early 1980s the Settle and Carlisle railway was still relatively busy with freight traffic. Most Anglo-Scottish wagonload consignments were routed this way with regular trains to and from Healey Mills, Tinsley, Bescot and Severn Tunnel Junction. On 20th July 1982, Class 47 No. 47076 'CITY OF TRURO' passes Settle Junction with 6S98, the 07.55 Severn Tunnel Junction–Mossend wagonload service. The main traffics carried are fuel oil in TTA tank wagons and domestic coal in MCV mineral wagons. In May 1983 the Settle and Carlisle line closed to through freight traffic, although local services continued for several more years to Ribblehead from the South and to Warcop and Newbiggin from the North.

Paul Shannon

Above: On Saturday 11th March 1989, when the West Coast main line was blocked by engineering work between Lancaster and Preston, several block steel trains to and from Mossend were diverted via Wennington, Settle Junction and Clitheroe. The trains were hauled over the diversionary route by pairs of Class 20s, hired from Railfreight Coal. Nos. 20028 and 20172 approach Settle Junction with the 6M24 Mossend–Dee Marsh Junction service, carrying hot rolled coil from Ravenscraig to Shotton. Today hot rolled coil is no longer dispatched from Ravenscraig, and the substitute flow of steel slabs from Ravenscraig to South Wales is firmly in the hands of pairs of refurbished Class 37s.

Paul Shannon

Class 370 vehicle No. 48107 leads a ten-car Advanced Passenger Train (APT) formation past Golborne Junction on 8th June 1984. This was during the period when the APT worked scheduled but unadvertised passenger trains between London Euston and Glasgow, and the service pictured here is the 16.30 departure from Euston. Two years later, the whole APT project was officially abandoned. Driving trailer No. 48107 made its final journey on BR metals on 24th June 1986 when it was towed along with nine other APT vehicles from Crewe to C.F. Booth's scrapyard at Rotherham. *Brian Roberts*

Class 90 No. 90026 hauls an (almost!) uniform rake of the InterCity-liveried stock past Coppull on 10th June 1989, forming the 14.36 service from Carlisle to London Euston. No. 90026 was the first member of the class to be outshopped in 'mainline' livery. Its days on main-line passenger services were to be short-lived, however, as it was reclassified into Railfreight Distribution's pool of 75 mph locomotives (sub-Class 90/1, pool MDMC) in July 1991. *Paul Shannon*

Above: Four features of this 1984 view at the south end of Bolton station have now passed into history – Bolton's semaphores, the fine LMS goods warehouse, the public freight terminal being served by a local trip working and, of course, the Class 45 locomotive in revenue-earning service. A consignment of finished steel, loaded on to BDA wagons, has just been shunted into the yard on 29th May by Class 45 No. 45051, forming the 6T85 trip working from Ashburys. It seems hard to believe now that on a typical weekday in 1984 BR would have operated three separate trip workings to the Bolton area – one to Bolton itself, one to Horwich, and one to Westhoughton.

Paul Shannon

The Trafford Park Estates railway came back to life in 1989 after a decade of dereliction. The first customer of the refurbished railway was Norton Metals, who dispatched a daily trainload of scrap metal to Cardiff, and further traffic was gained in 1990 when Cerestar started to send out wagonloads of starch to Sittingbourne, Thornton and Aberdeen. To cater for the new flows Trafford Park Estates acquired two Class 08 locomotives from BR. These were quickly repainted in the firm's green livery, but interestingly, their former BR numbers 08423 and 08669 were reapplied. No. 08669 negotiates one of the many public roads crossed by the railway with a light load of one PBA for Sittingbourne on 23rd August 1990. *Paul Shannon*

Railfreight gained some useful long-distance traffic in 1987 when the elderly coal hoists at Swansea were laid to rest and a new export terminal for Irish-bound coal was opened at Ellesmere Port. The Cawoods facility at Ellesmere Port receives regular trainloads of containerised coal both from South Wales and from the North East, hauled by Class 37/7 and Class 56 traction respectively. On 29th March 1988, revised blue-liveried Class 56 No. 56115 shunts a single PFA container flat at Ellesmere Port after arriving with a 'special' from Lynemouth colliery. *Brian Roberts*

Above: The heaviest petroleum trains out of Stanlow refinery are those to Leeds and Jarrow, comprising either fourteen bogie tanks or thirteen bogies and one four-wheeled tank. These trains are double-headed between Stanlow and Castleton. The train locomotive is almost always a Trainload Petroleum Class 47, and the assisting locomotive is normally a Class 37 or 47 from the same pool, although 'foreign' traction may appear from time to time. The 07.56 Stanlow–Jarrow tank train approaches Moore on 9th April 1990, with Trainload Petroleum Class 47 No. 47125 'Tonnidae' receiving assistance from departmental Class 47 No. 47333.

Paul Shannon

Right: Rapid fluctuations in the market for industrial fuel mean that many of the train services from Stanlow do not appear in the timetable but are operated as 'specials' when required. The ICI power station at Burn Naze, on the former Fleetwood branch is one of these locations which frequently changes its source of fuel, and recent years have seen trains run to Burn Naze from Stanlow, Immingham, Cardiff and Milford Haven. Waiting to join the main line at Poulton-le-Fylde is Class 47 No. 47193 'Lucinidae', with 7R37, the 14.00 Burn Naze–Stanlow empties on 12th April 1990.

Paul Shannon

For most of the 1980s Class 45 'Peaks' were a familiar sight on trans-Pennine passenger services, with western extensions to Liverpool and North Wales. Class 45/1 No. 45103 arrives at Warrington Bank Quay station with an afternoon Scarborough–Bangor train on 31st May 1985. This locomotive, like most of the others employed on trans-Pennine duties, had spent much of its earlier life hauling express passenger trains on the Midland line. In May 1987 the 'Peaks' gave way to Class 47s on remaining locomotive-hauled trains, and in January 1991 locomotive haulage ceased altogether in favour of Class 158 diesel multiple units. *Brian Denton*

The mid 1980s saw locomotive haulage return temporarily to many cross-country passenger services, before the full impact of 'Sprinterisation' was reached at the end of the decade. Perhaps the most exotic class to reach the North West on a regular basis was the Southern-based Class 33, which enjoyed regular diagrams to Manchester on services from Cardiff via Shrewsbury. Class 33 No. 33028 pulls into Stockport station with the 13.45 Manchester Piccadilly–Cardiff Central on 4th July 1985. These services later passed into the hands of Class 37/4 locomotives and eventually, with a few hiccoughs, into the hands of 'Sprinters'. *Paul Shannon*

Passenger traffic between London and Blackpool was buoyant enough to warrant the retention of direct trains throughout the 1980s, with the change from electric to diesel traction taking place at Preston. Class 47 No. 47478, still in blue livery despite its allocation to InterCity, passes Salwick signal box with the 12.25 London Euston–Blackpool North ser-

vice on 3rd September 1990. The train formation includes a driving va⟨trailer⟩ trailer at the rear, but this would be inoperative under diesel haulag⟨e⟩ and the train would be hauled conventionally back from Blackpool t⟨o⟩ Preston in due course.

Paul Shannon

The rickety signal box, semaphore signals and telegraph poles give a period feel to this photograph of Singleton, mid-way between Poulton and Kirkham on the principal route to the Fylde coast. The same cannot be said of the motive power, which is rather more in keeping with the photograph's date of 3rd September 1990. The train is 14.37 from Blackpool North to Stockport, formed of Class 150 three-car unit No. 150 233 and Class 150 two-car unit No. 150 249. 'Sprinters' such as these have brought increased efficiency to Fylde line operations, just as they have in other parts of the country, but in this case they were also used as a reason for frustrating BR's plans to electrify the route between Manchester and Blackpool.

Paul Shannon

Left: Class 86/4 No. 86424 was the second member of its class to receive red and grey Parcels livery, following an overhaul at Stratford in October 1990. The re-painting did not prevent No. 86424 from continuing to appear on passenger trains, and it is pictured here passing Grayrigg with the 12.00 Glasgow Central–London Euston service on 1st June 1991.

Paul Shannon

Right: Symbolising BR's corporate identity which prevailed throughout the 1970 and early 1980s blue-liveried Class 87 No. 87002 'Royal Sovereign' hauls a rake of blue and grey Mk 2A–F coaching stock past Low Gill on 31st May 1985, forming the 17.05 service from Glasgow Central to London Euston.

Andrew Vines

Left: The rounded peaks of the Howgill Fells from the backdrop to this view of Class 87 No. 87018 'Lord Nelson', descending from Grayrigg towards Oxenholme with the 11.28 Glasgow Central–Brighton service on 29th June 1991. This is one of the small number of trains routed via Kensington Olympia to provide a through service from the West Coast main line to the Southern Region, a route which BR virtually ignored until the May 1986 timetable change.

Paul Shannon

Right: Class 87 No. 87023 'Velocity' pauses at Preston in the pouring rain with the 17.35 London Euston–Glasgow Central service on 3rd December 1986. Apart from the obvious addition of overhead wires, the main part of Preston station has undergone little physical change in the last fifty years, and it remains a busy interchange point between the West Coast main line and secondary lines to Manchester, Blackpool, Colne and Ormskirk.

Andrew Vines

Wooden level crossing gates and a venerable signal box dating back to Lancashire & Yorkshire days survive at Parbold, where a two-car Class 108 unit, Nos. M 54502 and M 51917, is seen pulling away on an evening Southport–Manchester service on 8th May 1984. The Class 108 design has certainly stood the test of time, and units such as this one were still sharing Southport line duties with more modern 'Pacers' and 'Sprinters' in 1991.

Paul Shannon

Hellifield has survived the transition from a busy railway centre to a quiet rural backwater with much of its ornate ironwork intact, providing a welcome respite from the austere 'bus-shelter' image of many other unstaffed stations in the area. A call is made at Hellifield on 2nd June 1985 by four-car Class 110 DMU Nos. E 52070, E 51836, E 51824 and E 51845 – a total of 720 hp which would be more than adequate for the climb to Giggleswick! The train is the 17.17 departure from Leeds to Morecambe via Lancaster. For a short time in the late 1980s passengers on the Hellifield–Lancaster route enjoyed regular locomotive haulage, but by 1990 'Pacers' were the order of the day and there was talk of cutting back the already sparse train service.

Paul Shannon

Above: The first 'Pacer' units to enter squadron service west of the Pennines were the Class 142 vehicles for Manchester suburban services. To reflect their intended role, the first fourteen class 142s were painted in Greater Manchester's bright orange livery, through examples commonly strayed to other parts of the network. Unit No. 142 011 calls at Arnside on 23rd July 1990 while working the 19.12 Preston–Barrow local service.

Paul Shannon

Right: Perhaps the most embarrasing failure of the DMU replacement programme in the late 1980s was the attempt to introduce four-wheeled 'Pacer' vehicles to sharply curved branch lines in Cornwall. Thirteen Class 142s were delivered in Cornish chocolate and cream livery and named 'Skippers' in honour of their intended work, but severe flange wear and excessive squealing on curves led to their hasty transfer to Northern haunts in 1986/7. An unidentified chocolate and cream Class 142 unit approaches Greenfield on 20th July 1990, forming the 17.05 Leeds–Manchester Victoria service.

Paul Shannon

Left: The Cumbrian Coast line abounds in impressive scenery, especially on the central section from Workington to Whitehaven where the railway clings to a narrow belt of land between the Cumbrian hills and the Irish sea. Passing the village of Parton, just north of Whitehaven, is the daily Cumbrian Coast mail train, 1E01 17.53 Workington–Huddersfield, on 24th July 1990. Traction is provided by Class 31/4 No. 31413 'Severn Valley Railway', which carries the unique livery of rail blue with light blue bodyside stripes and red bands around the base of the cabs.

Paul Shannon

Above: Since the end of steam almost all passenger trains between Barrow and Carlisle have been formed of Class 108 units, specially fitted with window bars because of the restricted clearances on this stretch of line. In 1990 the Cumbrian Coast pool included vehicles Nos. 53964 and 54247, which had been repainted in original BR green (except for the obligatory yellow warning panels!) in 1986. These vehicles lead to a four-car Class 108 formation towards Nethertown on 24th July 1990, operating the 17.50 Barrow–Carlisle service.

Paul Shannon

Left: Problems with 'Pacer' gear boxes saw many of Manchester Class 142 units spending long periods out of service, and this led to Class 31-hauled replacement on a number of local routes. In summer 1990 there was one scheduled locomotive-hauled train around the Oldham loop in each direction on weekdays, linking up at Manchester Victoria with a service to and from Blackpool. Class 31 No. 31467 heads south from Shaw with the 09.40 Manchester–Rochdale–Oldham–Blackpool service on 6th July 1990. Most of the substitute locomotive-hauled trains in use at that time included Network SouthEast stock in the formation. *Paul Shannon*

Right: After 1985 the principal trans-Pennine route for freight traffic became the Calder Valley line via Hebden Bridge, with just a handful of chemicals and oil trains continuing to run via Diggle. The Diggle route saw a slight increase in traffic in January 1990, however, when Railfreight Distribution introduced a daytime Freightliner service between Crewe and Leeds. Class 47 No. 47005 crosses Saddleworth viaduct on 20th July 1990 with the return working, 4M40 1549 Leeds–Crewe. *Paul Shannon*

Left: In the early 1980s a number of Scottish Class 303 EMUs were transferred south to the Manchester area, and from 1984 onwards these units were repainted in the Greater Manchester livery of brown and orange. For a time their use was concentrated on the Manchester–Hadfield line, but by the end of the 1980s they were being used on a variety of services, including those to and from Altrincham. Unit No. 303 066 glides between Oxford Road and Piccadilly stations on 29th September 1989 whilst working the 13.10 Altrincham–Alderley Edge service. No. 303 066 was the last refurbished Class 303 unit to remain in service, its official withdrawal date being 11th March 1991.

John Hillmer

Right: For thirty-two years local services between Manchester Victoria and Bury were maintained by Class 504 EMUs. These bore visual similarities to other EMU builds of the late 1950s but were unique by virtue of their side-contact collection system from a third rail energised at 1200 volts D.C. Some Class 504s were placed in store as early as the 1970s, but the majority lived long enough to receive a repaint in Greater Manchester livery. The Class ended its revenue-earning career on BR in August 1991, when the Bury line was closed pending conversion to light rapid transit operation. On 17th March 1990, Class 504 cars Nos. M 77166 and M 65445 cross Radcliffe viaduct with the 15.00 service from Bury.

Paul Shannon

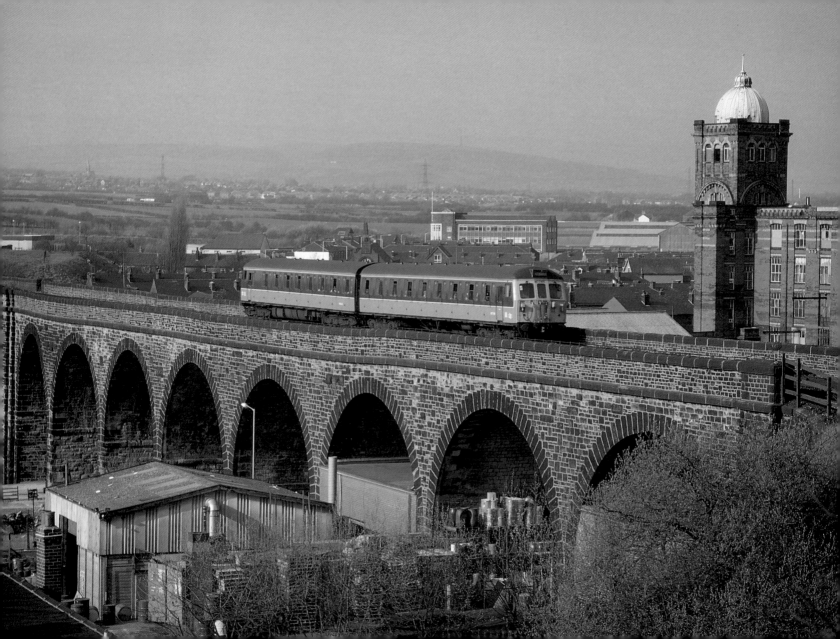

Left: Services on Merseyside network of d.c. electrified lines are operated today by Class 507 and Class 508 EMUs based at Hall Road and Birkenhead respectively. These units were amongst the first suburban EMU types to carry blue and grey livery – and also amongst the last to retain it! A pristine unit No. 507 003 calls at Freshfield station with the 15.35 departure from Southport on 10th May 1979.
Brian Denton

Above: Class 503 units dating back to the 1930s and 1950s survived in daily use on Wirral line services until the mid 1980s, when their duties were taken over by aluminium-bodied Class 508 units from the Southern Region. A six-car Class 503 formation, comprising vehicles Nos. M 28388, M 29829, M 29133, M 29156, M 29832 and M 28687, passes Birkenhead North No. 2 signal box with the 10.37 New Brighton–Liverpool Central service on 21st January 1982.
Paul Shannon

Shortly before sunset on 23rd July 1990, Class 31/4 No. 31426 clatters over Arnside viaduct with the 19.59 Barrow–Manchester Victoria service. No. 31426 was one of seven Class 31/4s transferred to Provincial pool PCDB in May 1990, helping to alleviate the shortage of serviceable second-generation DMUs in the North West.

Paul Shannon

In the final years of Speedlink, traffic for Trafford Park was conveyed by a daily service from Warrington, routed via Weaver Junction, Northwich and Stockport. The return service, 6F32 1809 Trafford Park–Warrington Arpley, is pictured on the former CLC route near Mobberley on 23rd August 1990, powered by Class 31 No. 31146. The consist included two ferry wagons for mainland Europe via Dover and one bogie starch tank for Thornton Junction, all of which would travel forward from Warrington on overnight trunk Speedlink services. After July 1991 Trafford Park continued to receive wagonload traffic to and from Europe, but the trip from Warrington was replaced by a shared Freightliner/wagonload service from Crewe. *Paul Shannon*

Right: The 1980s saw a major growth in up-market excursion trains, and not surprisingly the Settle to Carlisle line was high on the list of favoured routes. Class 47 No. 47627 'City of Oxford' approaches Grisedale crossing, north of Garsdale, with the return leg of the Cumbrian Mountain Pullman on 20th June 1987. Northbound the train had been hauled by Bulleid West Country Class No. 34092 'CITY OF WELLS'. The rolling stock includes former East Coast Pullmans built by Metropolitan-Cammell in 1960/1 and sold to SLOA for charter train work in 1981.

Andrew Vines

Above: The Castle cement works at Horrocksford Junction, Clitheroe sent out regular trainloads of cement to Gunnie, Newcastle and Middlesbrough in the 1980s. Class 47 No. 47380 crosses Gisburn viaduct on 5th August 1987 with the evening departure to the North East, which could serve either Newcastle or Middlesbrough as required. By 1989 the practice of running a separate train to the North East had ceased, and traffic for Newcastle and Middlesbrough was conveyed by the Gunnie service as far as Carlisle, with onward connections via Hexham. Since the Gunnie train ran via Blackburn this left the Clitheroe–Hellifield line without any regular freight service.

Andrew Vines

Above: The West Coast main line remains an important artery for parcels and mail traffic. An InterCity-liveried Class 86 locomotive passes Winwick Junction on 23rd May 1990 with 1S81, the 1759 Birmingham New Street–Glasgow Central mail train. *Paul Shannon*

Right: Bolton's single parcels platform became a hive of activity after the May 1990 timetable change when three services were diverted to start from Bolton instead of Manchester Piccadilly. Class 47 No. 47522 'Doncaster Enterprise' shunts vans for the first departure of the day, 1V03 14.23 Bolton–Cardiff Central, on 18th August 1990. The other new services were 1C35, the 16.25 to London St Pancras and 1V05, the 18.31 to Cardiff Central. No 47522 was the seventh member of its class to receive Parcels red and grey livery, having been outshopped from Doncaster in its new colours in July 1990. *Paul Shannon*

Above: Class 20s have been associated with Fiddlers Ferry coal traffic since the mid 1980s, with regular workings to and from Bickershaw, Parkside, Point of Ayr, Silverdale and Hem Heath collieries, plus short-term use on trains of imported coal from Gladstone Dock. 'Old' Rail-freight-liveried Class 20 No. 20175 and blue-liveried 20182 head north near Winwick on 21st May 1990 with empty HAAs for Wigan, whilst another pair – Nos. 20131 and 20154 – head south with a loaded train from Bickershaw. Class 60s were introduced on Gladstone Dock–Fiddlers Ferry coal trains in summer 1991 and were expected to replace Class 20s on other services to Fiddlers Ferry by the end of the year.   *Paul Shannon*

Right: Class 20 locomotives Nos. 20143 and 20130 pass Crosfield's Crossing signal box on the approach to Warrington with 6T76 Fiddlers Ferry–Wigan merry-go-round empties on 8th September 1990. The freight-only line between Warrington and Ditton is mechanically signalled throughout, and three of its signal boxes are situated within half a mile of each other at Monks Siding, Litton's Mill and Crosfield's Crossing.

Paul Shannon

Left The British Steel plant at Workington provides Trainload Metals with regular inward block trains of steel slabs from Lackenby and less regular outward consignments of steel rail. Until July 1991 much of the steel rail was carried out by the daily Speedlink service from Workington to Willesden. Class 47 No. 47245 winds through Harrington on 24th July 1990 with 6A40, the 16.40 Workington–Willesden, conveying one YAA and YLA one wagons with steel rail for BR use. The train would call at Corkickle to collect chemical tanks before continuing its journey round the Cumbrian Coast.

Paul Shannon

Above Closure of Haig colliery at Whitehaven in the mid 1980s left the Cumbrian Coast line with just one source of coal traffic, the opencast disposal point at Maryport. Class 47 No. 47365 'ICI Diamond Jubilee' crosses Eskmeals viaduct with the daily Maryport–Rugeley merry-go-round on 30th May 1989. Class 47 motive power was the norm for this train until July 1991, when Class 60s took over.

Andrew Vines

Left: RMC's Dove Holes quarry provides a characteristic Peak District backdrop to Class 60 No 60058 'John Howard' as it backs a rake of 23 JHA hopper wagons into the loading area on 10th July 1991. The train had just returned empty from Manchester as 6H60, the 08.40 Hope Street–Peak Forest, and the wagons would now be reloaded in time to form the afternoon train to Washwood Heath. No. 60058 was on temporary loan to Buxton for crew training purposes: its subsector decals indicate that it will ultimately form part of the Trainload Coal fleet, working from either Toton or Wigan Springs Branch.

Paul Shannon

Right: Pairs of refurbished Class 37s were introduced to Buxton area stone workings in early 1987. Thirteen locomotives were allocated to this traffic, and these were based for maintenance purposes at Tinsley until their transfer to Immingham (pool FABI) in September 1990. Routine 'A' and 'B' examinations, however, have always been carried out locally at Buxton. Class 37s Nos. 37686 and 37676 head east between Edale and Hope with 6E68, the 09.13 Peak Forest–Selby, on 10th July 1991. The summer 1991 timetable showed two booked services each week from Peak Forest to Selby, though extra trains could be laid on if required by the customer.

Paul Shannon

Designed to bring InterCity standards of air-conditioned comfort to cross-country routes, the Class 158 marked the final stage of the 'Sprinter revolution' of the 1980s and early 1990s. In the North West, Class 158 units ousted the last remaining locomotive-hauled trains on the Diggle route in January 1991, and they also found employment on services between Liverpool and York via the Calder Valley. Unit No. 158 749 calls at Newton-le-Willows on 25th May 1991, forming the 10.57 stopping train from Liverpool Lime Street to York.

Paul Shannon

As a prelude to the reintroduction of 'Club' trains to Southport and Blackpool in July 1991, Regional Railways started a Class 37 crew familiarisation programme on 13th May, with one locomotive rostered to work the Southport service until 7th June and the Blackpool service from 10th June until 5th July. The chosen locomotive was Class 37/4 No. 37430, allocated to Railfreight Distribution pool FDET and based at Tinsley. This locomotive is pictured pulling into Burscough Bridge station with the 17.06 Manchester Victoria–Southport service on 4th June.

Paul Shannon

With Fiddlers Ferry power station on the skyline, Class 37/7 No. 37803 heads south on the West Coast Main Line near Daresbury with 6V07, the 07.45 Ellesmere Port–Radyr coal empties, on Saturday 9th November 1991. This train had been amended to run via Warrington, with reversal at Bank Quay station after the fire at West Cheshire Junction signal box which led to closure of the freight-only West Cheshire Junction–Mouldsworth line.

Paul Shannon